Pulleys

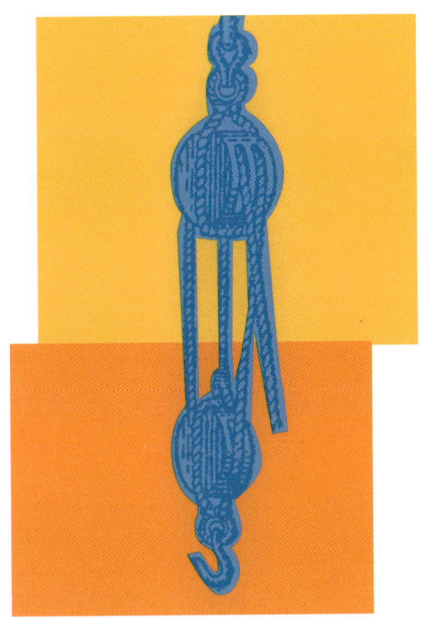

A Buddy Book
by
Sarah Tieck

VISIT US AT
www.abdopublishing.com

Published by ABDO Publishing Company, 4940 Viking Drive, Edina, Minnesota 55435.

Copyright © 2007 by Abdo Consulting Group, Inc. International copyrights reserved in all countries. No part of this book may be reproduced in any form without written permission from the publisher. Buddy Books™ is a trademark and logo of ABDO Publishing Company.

Printed in the United States.

Contributing Editor: Michael P. Goecke
Graphic Design: Maria Hosley
Cover Photograph: Photos.com, Clipart.com
Interior Photographs/Illustrations: Clipart.com, DigitalVision, ImageBank, Photodisc, Photos.com

Library of Congress Cataloging-in-Publication Data

Tieck, Sarah, 1976–
   Pulleys / Sarah Tieck.
      p. cm. — (Simple machines)
   Includes index.
   ISBN-13: 978-1-59679-815-1
   ISBN-10: 1-59679-815-7
 1. Pulleys—Juvenile literature. I. Title. II. Series: Tieck, Sarah, 1976- Simple machines.

TJ1103.T54 2006
621.8–dc22
                                                                                2006010044

Table Of Contents

What Is A Pulley? 4

Parts Of A Pulley 8

How Does A Pulley Work? 10

Different Pulleys At Work 12

The History Of Pulleys 16

**How Do Pulleys Help
People Today?** 20

Web Sites 22

Important Words 23

Index 24

What Is A Pulley?

Pulleys are used to lift or move things. A pulley is a simple machine. A simple machine has few moving parts, sometimes only one.

Simple machines give people a **mechanical advantage**. This is how pulleys help make work easier for people.

Many sailors use pulleys to raise and lower the sails of ships.

Pulleys are not the only simple machines. There are six simple machines. These include pulleys, wedges, levers, screws, inclined planes, and wheels and axles.

Sometimes, simple machines work together. Most machines are made up of more than one simple machine. Pulleys are used in flagpoles, cranes, and elevators.

simple machines

Inclined Planes
Help move objects.

Levers
Help lift or move objects.

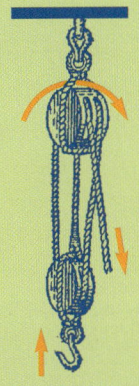

Pulleys
Help move, lift, and lower objects.

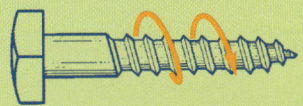

Screws
Help lift, lower, and fasten objects.

Wedges
Help fasten or split objects.

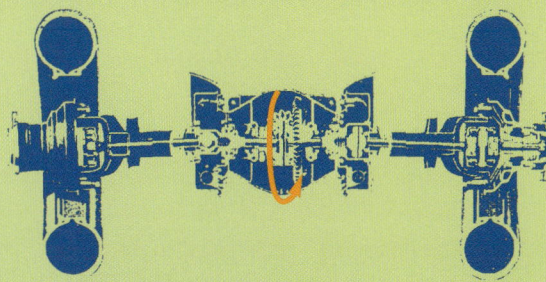

Wheels and Axles
Help move objects.

7

Parts of a Pulley

Pulleys give people a **mechanical advantage**. The parts of a pulley work together to help people lift things.

In a pulley, there is a wheel. This helps to support the **load**. There is also a rope or a chain in a pulley. This helps to move the load.

There is a **groove** in the wheel. This helps to hold the rope or chain in place.

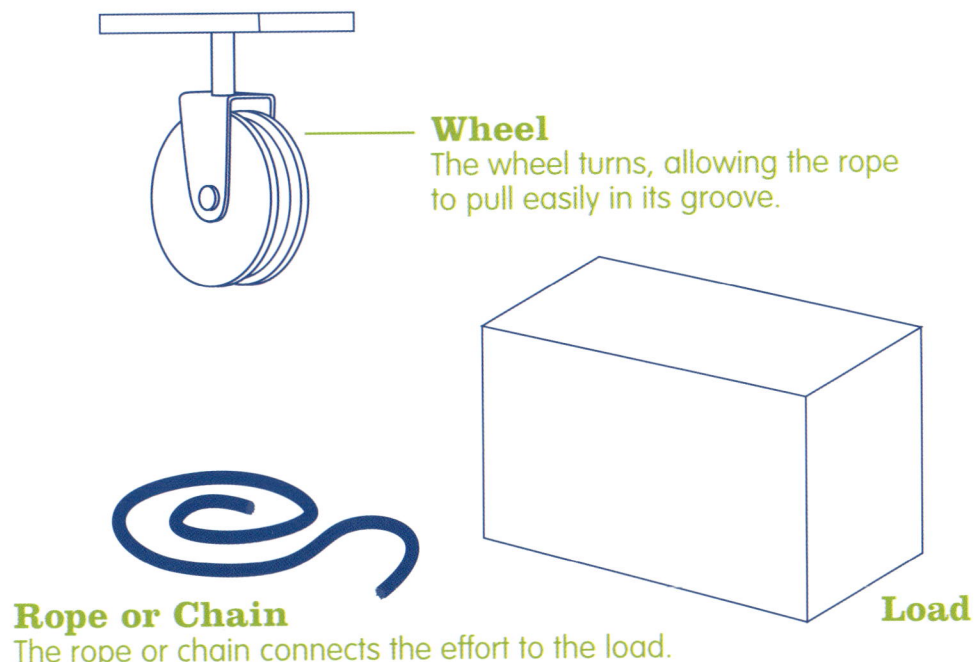

Wheel
The wheel turns, allowing the rope to pull easily in its groove.

Rope or Chain
The rope or chain connects the effort to the load.

Load

Last, there is a **load**. This is the object that needs to be lifted or moved. The load is located on one end of the rope. It supplies **resistance**.

Someone or something must supply **effort** on the other end of the rope. This is how the load will be lifted or moved.

How Does A Pulley Work?

It is not easy for a person to lift something heavy, such as a big box, on his or her own. But, a person could lift a box with a pulley.

A pulley makes work easier. It changes how heavy something feels to lift. A pulley gives a person a **mechanical advantage**. By using more pulleys, the job requires less **effort**.

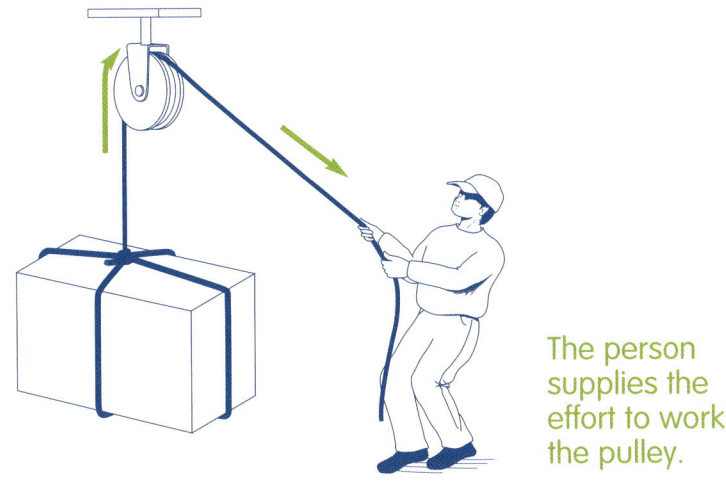

The person supplies the effort to work the pulley.

To use a pulley to move a box, a person would tie one end of a rope around the box. Then, he or she would slide the other end of the rope into the pulley's **groove**.

The person will hold the end of the rope farthest from the box. To move the box, he or she will pull down on the rope. By doing this, the person is applying **force**. This action helps move or lift the weight of the box.

Different Pulleys At Work

There are many ways to change how a pulley works. Different pulleys help people move different **loads**.

Pulleys can be fixed. This means they stay in one place. Pulleys can also be movable.

Pulleys help to move elevators up and down.

This movable pulley is helping to make the work of lifting this object easier.

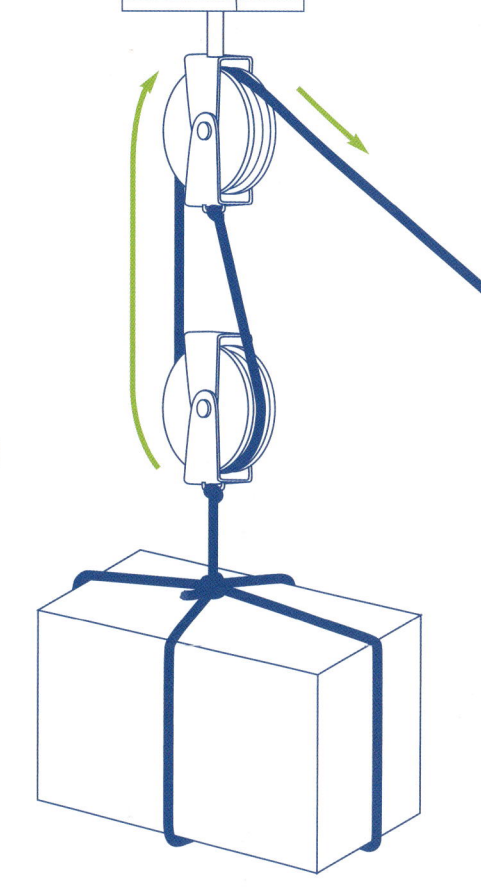

It is possible to change the way a pulley works by using more than one pulley. By using multiple pulleys, the **load** feels lighter and becomes easier to lift. This is called a compound pulley. Less **force** is needed with a compound pulley.

The History of Pulleys

The pulley has been used for many years. Ancient people used pulleys. But, a Greek mathematician named Archimedes was one of the first to write about this simple machine.

▲ Greek mathematician Archimedes did many experiments to learn about pulleys.

In Archimedes's time, people didn't have machines with motors. People had to do the work with their bodies. Archimedes helped them understand how to use pulleys to make work easier.

Archimedes was famous for his ideas. He knew a lot about mathematics and science. He was always experimenting with formulas and theories. Many times, he discovered tools that helped people. Some of his tools and ideas are still used today.

Since ancient times, pulleys have helped people lift loads with their bodies.

How Do Pulleys Help People Today?

Today, people have many types of tools. But, they still use pulleys.

When you fish with a fishing pole, you are using a pulley. When you see someone use a wrecking ball and a crane, you are watching him or her use a pulley. When you raise a flag up a flagpole, you are using another type of pulley.

▲ A fishing pole uses a pulley to help reel in fish.

A pulley on a crane is very useful on a construction site.

Pulleys help with many different jobs all over the world.

Web Sites

To learn more about **Pulleys**, visit ABDO Publishing Company on the World Wide Web. Web site links about **Pulleys** are featured on our Book Links page. These links are routinely monitored and updated to provide the most current information available.

www.abdopublishing.com

Important Words

effort an attempt to lift or move something.

force a push or pull against resistance.

groove a long, narrow channel cut into something.

load an object that needs to be turned, lifted, or moved.

mechanical advantage the way simple machines make work easier. Using a simple machine to help with a task means less, or different, effort is needed to do a job. The same job would require more effort without the help of a simple machine.

resistance something that works against or opposes.

Index

Archimedes 16, 17, 18

box 10, 11

chain 8, 9

crane 6, 20, 22

effort 9, 10, 11

elevator 6, 13

fish 20, 21

fishing pole 20, 21

flag 20

flagpole 6, 20

force 11, 15

groove 8, 9, 11

inclined plane 6, 7

lever 6, 7

load . . . 8, 9, 12, 15, 19

resistance 9

rope 8, 9, 11

sail 5

screw 6, 7

ships 5

wedge 6, 7

wheel 6, 7, 8, 9

wheel and axle 6, 7

wrecking ball 20